HOME COUNTS

7

SOLUTIONS FOR BURNED-OUT PARENTS

DR. JAMES DOBSON

Multnomah® Publishers Sisters, Oregon

7 SOLUTIONS FOR BURNED-OUT PARENTS
published by Multnomah Publishers, Inc.

© 2004 by James Dobson, Inc.
International Standard Book Number: 1-59052-385-7
Cover image of family by age fotostock.
Cover image of mother and child by Photolibrary.com/Photonica

Unless otherwise indicated, Scripture quotations are from:
The Holy Bible, New International Version
© 1973, 1984 by International Bible Society,
used by permission of Zondervan Publishing House

Other Scripture quotations are from:
The Holy Bible, King James Version (KJV)
Holy Bible, New Living Translation (NLT)
© 1996. Used by permission of Tyndale House Publishers, Inc.

Printed in the United States of America

For information:
MULTNOMAH PUBLISHERS, INC.
POST OFFICE BOX 1720
SISTERS, OREGON 97759

04 05 06 07 08 09 10—10 9 8 7 6 5 4 3 2 1 0

Dedication

This book is affectionately dedicated to today's mothers and fathers who are burdened by the never-ending pressures and obligations of living. The resultant stress and exhaustion have become the universal malady among families in Western nations. It is my prayer that the ideas and suggestions I have offered in *7 Solutions* will help to lighten the load and encourage parents to give priority to the precious boys and girls entrusted to their care. When these breathless years have slid into history, it will be evident that the task of raising children in the fear and admonition of the Lord was the responsibility that mattered most. May God grant daily wisdom and strength with each step along the journey.

Now, put aside your to-do list, make yourself a cup of tea, sit in a comfortable chair or a warm bath, and enjoy reading along with me. The world will wait while you do.

Contents

Acknowledgments

I especially want to express appreciation to my editor, Jim Lund, for his invaluable assistance in helping to research, compile, and shape the material in this book.

Thanks also go to Jennifer Gott, Pamela McGrew, and all of my friends at Multnomah who played a role in this important project.

Introduction

Kay and Leonard often long for a simpler life. Their three kids play on soccer, basketball, and baseball teams, take piano and swimming lessons, and attend Boy Scouts and the weekly church youth program—and that's on top of a full load of schoolwork and extra projects. When Kay isn't transporting her children to various activities, she volunteers at their school and at church. Leonard isn't available to help much—he's fighting to catch up at work, frequently putting in overtime on weekdays and weekends.

Though Kay has given up her home business

to have more time for her family, she still feels overwhelmed.

"Yesterday I drove the kids into town four times," she said recently. "By the time the day was over, all I had done other than chauffur them around was stop at the store for a bag of cat food. It's crazy." She admits to being exhausted and discouraged most days and feels that something needs to change. But there is little time to reflect on what—the next event is always just a few minutes away.

Another mother, Angela, maintains a similarly hectic schedule. After a full day at the office, she spends so much time driving her children to programs and practices that her one-year-old, when away from the family minivan, seems "somewhat disoriented."

Is your life at all like Kay, Leonard, and Angela's? Are you also running in endless circles, tired and depressed, too busy to read a good book or take a long walk with your spouse or hold your toddler in your lap while telling him or her a story? Have you eliminated almost every meaningful activity in order to deal with the tyranny of a never-ending "to do" list?

Do your children feel more at ease in the

family car than in your own home?

If so, you're not alone. This overcommitted and breathless existence, which I call "routine panic," is one of the tragedies of family life in the twenty-first century. Everyone seems to be caught up in the "rat race." As we hurtle through our days, our lives increasingly resemble runaway freight trains.

Want to get off the train before it crashes? Even in this hectic, hurry-up society, it *is* possible to slow the pace of life enough to enjoy each day, to nurture your marriage and family, and to develop a deep and meaningful relationship with the Lord. It's not easy, but with even a few positive steps you can start moving away from life as a burned-out parent and toward a more fulfilling life of peace and rest.

My prayer is that this book, the first in my new Home Counts series, will provide the encouragement and practical advice you need to accomplish that. It draws from the same time-tested, biblically based concepts and material that I have presented to families for many years. The text primarily addresses married couples, but it applies just as much to harried single parents.

The seven "solutions" presented are not the

only means to a more relaxed mode of living—but from my observations and experience, they are a great place to start. I hope you will give these suggestions a try, along with the tips at the end of each chapter. After all, anything has to be better than raising your family in a minivan!

1

The Sacred Rhythm of Rest

"Be still, and know that I am God."

PSALM 46:10

We all need rest to thrive. It's not just a convenience that we try to squeeze into our schedules or an indulgence for those who aren't willing to work hard. Regular times of quiet and stillness are a spiritual and biological necessity. Many members of the animal kingdom, as well as certain plant species, will hibernate or lie dormant through the winter months in order to survive. We humans have a much harder time acknowledging the natural rhythms of life.

One of those humans, a bewildered new dad named Jack, once wrote me a letter asking for advice. Here is part of that note (the italics are mine):

> The Lord has blessed us so much, and I should be full of joy. But I have been depressed for about ten months now. I don't know whether to turn to a pastor, a physician, a psychologist, a nutritionist, or a chiropractor.
>
> Last September the Lord blessed us with a beautiful baby boy. He is just wonderful. We can't help but love him. *But he has been very demanding.* The thing that made it hardest for me was last semester Margie was taking classes three nights a week to finish her BA degree, and I took care of little Danny. He cried and sobbed the whole time we were together. I was used to being able to pay my bills, work out the budget, read, file mail, answer letters, type lists, etc., in the evening, but all this had to be postponed until Margie was here.
>
> I got very tired and started having a great deal of trouble getting up to go to work. I really should be at work at 8, but

I haven't been there before 9 or 9:30 in months. *It seems like I'm always fighting the flu.*

I don't understand why I'm so depressed. Sure, Margie gets tired because we can't seem to get Danny to bed before 11 or 12 midnight and he wakes up twice per night to be fed. But she's not depressed. *All this getting awakened at night really gets to me.*

Another thing that has been a constant struggle is leaving Danny in the nursery at church. He isn't content to be away from us very long, so they end up having to track Margie down almost every Sunday. *We hardly ever get to be together.*

There are a few other things that probably contribute to my depression. They are (1) responsibilities at work—we're short-handed and I'm trying to do too much; (2) spending too many weekends with yard work or trying to fix up our fixer-upper house; and (3) our finances, which are very limited. We don't want Margie to go to work, so we are on a meticulous budget. It's down to the bare essentials now.

We have all the things we would ever dream of at our age (twenty-seven): our own neat little house in a good neighborhood, a job I consider a ministry. We have a fine healthy boy, each other, and not least of all, our life in Christ.

I have no reason to be depressed and tired all the time. I come home from work so exhausted that I don't even want Danny near me. If you have any insights as to what I should do, please let me know. Thanks and God bless you.

Jack

This young father is well on the way to burning out. When one looks at his impossible schedule, it is no surprise that his mind and body are rebelling. After handling an extremely demanding job, he comes home to a fussy baby, a wife in night school, and mountains of bills and paperwork to do. On weekends he is rebuilding his rundown house. Finally, Jack made it clear that he and his wife have no time alone together, no fun in their lives, no social life, no regular exercise, and no escape from the baby. No wonder!

In addition to these other pressures, Jack can't even get an uninterrupted night's sleep. He climbs into bed about midnight, but is awakened at least twice before morning. That is probably the key to his depression. Some individuals are extremely vulnerable to loss of sleep, and this man appears to be one of them.

I am another. Our son, Ryan, did not sleep through the night once in his first four months, and I thought I was going to die. There is no sound on earth quite like the piercing screech of an infant in the wee hours of the morning. People who say they "sleep like a baby" probably never had one!

The human body will not tolerate this kind of pressure for long. And when one's body is exhausted, an interesting thing happens to the emotions. They also malfunction. You see, the mind, body, and spirit are very close neighbors. One usually catches the ills of the other. You'll recall that Jack did not understand his depression. He had every reason to be happy, yet he was miserable. Why? Because his depleted physical condition greatly affected his mental apparatus. And if the truth were known, his spiritual life probably wasn't all that inspiring either.

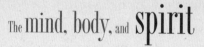

The mind, body, and spirit are very close neighbors.

The three departments of our intellect are tightly linked; they tend to move up and down as a unit. This is why it is so important for us to maintain and support the triad: mind, body, and spirit. If one breaks down, the entire engine begins to sputter.

Wayne Muller, in his book *Sabbath: Restoring the Sacred Rhythm of Rest,* relates what a physician once told him:

> I discovered in medical school that the more exhausted I was, the more tests I would order. I was too tired to see precisely what was going on with my patients. I could recognize their symptoms and formulate possible diagnoses, but I couldn't hear precisely how it fit together....
>
> But when I was rested, I could rely on my intuition and experience to tell

me what was needed. If there was any uncertainty, I would order a specific test to confirm my diagnosis. But when I was rested and could listen, I was almost always right.[1]

We perform best when we are not over-loaded, hurried, and sleep-deprived. That is simply how the human system works, and it is no accident. The Lord designed and created us to function this way. He knows everything about how our bodies work, right down to the tiniest atom. He also fully understands our overzealous tendencies and how easy it is for us to put off regular periods of renewal. This must be why He set an example of *rest* for us at the very beginning of human history and why He commands us to put aside a day each week to relax, pray, and reju-venate.

A Holy Day of Rest

God introduced the concept of the Sabbath at the time of Creation, after He formed the world in six days:

By the seventh day God had finished the work he had been doing; so on the seventh day he rested from all his work. And God blessed the seventh day and made it holy, because on it he rested from all the work of creating that he had done.

GENESIS 2:2-3

I don't believe the Ruler of the universe *needed* rest after creating the world. No effort is too taxing for the Lord. Rather, He wanted to emphasize the significance of the Sabbath right from the start.

God spelled out exactly how He expects us to respond to the Sabbath—and how important it is to Him—when He included it in the law given to Moses as the Ten Commandments:

"Remember the Sabbath day by keeping it holy. Six days you shall labor and do all your work, but the seventh day is a Sabbath to the LORD your God. On it you shall not do any work, neither you, nor your son or daughter, nor your manservant or maidservant, nor your animals, nor the alien within your gates.

For in six days the LORD made the heavens and the earth, the sea, and all that is in them, but he rested on the seventh day. Therefore the LORD blessed the Sabbath day and made it holy."

EXODUS 20:8–11

The Sabbath is to be a holy time, devoid of work and dedicated to worship, prayer, and praise. When we honor God by setting aside phone calls, e-mails, bill paying, and laundry in order to reflect on Him and spend quiet time together as a family, we begin to sense the depth of the restoring love, peace, and power that are available to us.

Black Sunday

In the Dobson household, we have attempted to observe the Sabbath over the years, choosing to worship in church whenever possible and not attend professional athletic events, go skiing, or attend movies on what we call "the Lord's day." I wish I could say, however, that we have been that disciplined with regard to doing paperwork or handling our other professional responsibilities on Sunday. That would not be truthful. But to the extent that we have violated our own ethics, we have always felt guilty about it and wish that we had been more careful to follow the plan for healthy living given to us by the Lord.

It seems at times that even the obligations of raising a family conspired to make the "day of rest" a time of stress. Especially when our children were young, Sunday mornings could actually become our most frustrating time of the week. I recall one of those mornings, which we now refer to as "Black Sunday." Have you ever had an experience like this one?

We began that day by getting up too late, meaning everyone had to rush to get to church on time. That produced emotional pressure, especially for Shirley and me. Then there was the matter of spilt milk at breakfast and the black shoe polish on the floor. And, of course, our son Ryan got dressed first, enabling him to slip out the back door and get himself dirty from head to toe. It was necessary to take him down to the skin and start over with clean clothes once more.

Instead of handling these irritants as they arose, we began criticizing one another and hurling accusations back and forth. At least one spanking was delivered, and another three or four were promised. Finally, four harried people managed to stumble into church. There's not a pastor in the world who could have moved us that morning.

My point is that you, too, will struggle at times as you attempt to set aside a day of rest each week for your family. There will be occasions when your Sunday is anything but calm and rejuvenating. Emergencies and unavoidable conflicts with work schedules may force you to observe your Sabbath on a different day altogether.

Do not permit these temporary obstacles and failures to discourage you! The principle of the Sabbath is more important to the Lord than the letter of the law. Christ Himself allowed the disciples to pick heads of grain on the Sabbath (Mark 2:23–27) and repeatedly healed the sick on God's holy day, to the consternation of the Pharisees (Mark 3:1–6; Luke 13:10–17; 14:1–6; John 5:1–9; 9:1–41). Jesus was more concerned about doing good (Mark 3:4) than adhering to the Pharisees' legalistic interpretation of what constituted a proper Sabbath.

Yet Jesus clearly understood the value of spiritual renewal and rest. He once invited the disciples to "Come with me by yourselves to a quiet place and get some rest" (Mark 6:31). Even when crowds of people approached Him to be healed, He "often withdrew to lonely places and prayed" (Luke 5:16).

Take a break each week to relax, spend time with God, and study His Word.

Sharpening Our Tools

If Jesus, for whom anything was possible, chose repeatedly in the midst of His great teaching to withdraw to quiet places for rest and conversation with His Father, how much more do each of us need to do the same? Though our modern culture will continually tempt you to do otherwise, you will find that taking a break each week to relax, spend time with God, and study His Word will leave you a more refreshed and effective parent. Likewise, keeping the Lord's day will provide a much-needed physical, emotional, and spiritual benefit to your spouse and children.

Preacher and author Charles Spurgeon once penned this remarkable statement about the value of Sabbath rest:

> Look at the mower in the summer's day. With so much to cut down before the sun sets, he pauses in his labor. Is he a sluggard? He looks for a stone and begins to draw it up and down his scythe, rink a tink, rink a tink, rink a tink. He's sharpening his blade. Is that idle music? Is he wasting precious moments? How much he might have mown while he was ringing out those notes on his blade. But he is sharpening his tool. And he will do far more, when once again he gives his strength to those long sweeps which lay the grass prostrate in rows before him. Even thus a little pause prepares the mind for greater service in a good cause.
>
> Fishermen must mend their nets and we must, every now and then, repair our mental states and set our machinery in order for future service. It is wisdom to

take occasional furloughs. In the long
run, we shall do more by sometimes
doing less.[2]

In our fast-paced world, taking a day to rest
and refresh is more than a luxury—it is essential
to our success as marriage partners and parents.
The best reason for observing the Sabbath, however, is that it places us firmly in God's will,
pleasing Him and bringing Him glory. No reward
is greater than that.

Worn Out? Too Busy?
Solution #1
Renew the Sabbath

- Talk with your family—how can you make your Sabbath a holy day? You might start by unplugging the telephone and beginning each new activity with a prayer.

- What steps can you take the day before your Sabbath—such as paying the bills, catching up the dishes and laundry, or making sure the kids finish homework—to make your day of rest more relaxing?

- On your Sabbath, choose a book or section of the Bible to read; then take a leisurely walk and allow God to speak to you.

Having It All

There is a time for everything,
and a season for every activity under heaven.

ECCLESIASTES 3:1

It occurred when I was thirty-three years old and was writing my first book. I was running at incredible speed, working myself to death like every other man I knew. I was superintendent of youth for my church and labored under a heavy speaking schedule. Eight or ten "unofficial" responsibilities were added to my full-time commitment at USC School of Medicine and Children's Hospital of Los Angeles. I once worked seventeen nights straight without being home in the evening. Danae, our five-year-old daughter, would stand in the doorway and cry as I left in the morning, knowing she might not see me until the sunrise.

Although my activities were bringing me professional advancement and the trappings of financial success, my dad was not impressed. He had observed my hectic lifestyle and felt obligated to express his concern. While flying from Los Angeles to Hawaii one summer, he used that quiet opportunity to write me a lengthy and loving letter, gently expressing how great a mistake it would be if I continued to pour every resource into my career and failed to meet my obligations to my wife and daughter. This is what he wrote:

> Dear Jimbo: It's been some time since I wrote you a fatherly letter, or any letters of any kind. It is worthy of note, I think, that of all the scores of communications that go to make up our total correspondence, including those of your high school and college days, I can recall no letter that ever had to be written in anger or even in a mild reprimand, and none, from this vantage point, that isn't accompanied by a nostalgic aura of pleasantness. In a word today, I feel more than ever like saying that it's been great to be your father, though the success of the relation-

ship, on mature reflection, seems far more the result of your relation to me, rather than any excellence on my part. I'm proud to be a member of the team.

My prayer and hope and expectation is that the same reverential affinity under God will always exist between you and your children. I'm very sure that love and faith in the living Christ are always the only cornerstones and building blocks for the making of memories that bless rather than burst. I'm very happy about your success, which is now coming in like showers. It is important for men in all vocations to experience the realization of their dreams. At this point, you have had a very high ratio of positive returns on your endeavors, almost unbelievable, in fact.

I don't need to remind you that it won't always be so. Life will test you deeply, if only in the ultimate, when we have to lay down everything. To this point, you have been untested, but trials are inevitable. If frustration and heartbreak do not come relative to your career, you must mentally prepare for it in some other areas. I know this is largely impossible to do in a day of sunshine and roses. "Sufficient unto the day is the evil thereof," but we should also add, "only for those who keep a strong hold on God through the happy times."

We must all pray definitely, pointedly, and continuously for your daughter. She is growing up in the wickedest section of the world, much farther gone into moral decline than the world into which you were born. I have observed that one of the greatest delusions is to suppose that children will be devout Christians simply because their parents have been, or that any of them will enter into life in any other way than through the valley of deep travail of prayer and faith. Failure at this point from you would make mere success in business a very pale and washed-out affair indeed, but this prayer demands time, time that cannot be given if it is all signed and conscripted and laid on the altar of career ambition.

In my case, there was a happy coincidence of my career as a minister with the care of your soul, and I'm without regret that the modest appointments that were mine to fill in your childhood offered me the time needed to pray for you. In your case, it will have to be done by design—jealously guarded, conscious design. The future—all the future—is ultimately all brightness for any Christian, and today mine looks particularly bright. But the tragedy of a child who is made shipwrecked of faith in life can mar the old age of anyone, Christian or otherwise. We must all work together to achieve for you the serenity which is mine in this respect, as I enter the youth of my old age. That is only one more reason we should all drink to the full the cup that is in our hands.

Those words shook me to the core and made me reexamine my priorities.

Dr. Gary Rosberg, founder of America's Family Coaches, once experienced a similar revelation. While studying for his doctoral degree,

Gary was interrupted by his five-year-old daughter, Sarah. She showed him a picture of their family: Sarah, her little sister, their mom, and the family dog, Katie. She even had a title for it: Our Family Best.

But something made Gary uneasy. Something was missing from the picture.

"Sarah," Gary asked, not sure if he wanted to hear the answer, "where is your daddy?"

"You're at the library," she said.

It was a moment that stopped time. Gary's head swirled as he realized how disconnected he was from his family. He resolved right then to become a more active participant in his children's lives, regardless of the cost to his professional ambitions.[3]

The lure of career advancement, and the ego satisfaction that comes with it, is not restricted to men, of course. Since the arrival of feminism and the sexual revolution in the 1960s, thousands of women have joined the labor force wholeheartedly. They have earned new levels of financial and emotional independence—but in the case of mothers, it has come at a cost.

Helen Gurley Brown, in her 1982 book *Having It All*, advised women that it is possible to achieve multiple competing goals without having to make tough choices. She is wrong, except in rare cases. I *am* sympathetic to the frustrations and pressures that lead mothers to work outside the home. I also understand that many women today must draw a paycheck simply to make ends meet. But when the demand for energy exceeds the supply, *for whatever reason,* exhaustion is inevitable. And children are almost always the losers in the competition for that limited resource.

Career ambition is not the only pursuit that can draw us away from our families, of course. Seemingly benign activities such as working out at the gym, golfing, fishing, hunting, going shopping, making home improvements, or volunteering at school or church are actually harmful if they consume every ounce of energy, leaving us utterly spent and incapable of focusing on our spouse and children.

When the demand for energy exceeds the supply, for whatever reason, exhaustion is inevitable.

Energy Crisis

The best book I have read on this subject is entitled *Parent Burnout* (now out of print), by Dr. Joseph Procaccini and Mark Kiefaber.[4] The authors describe how parents manage to squander their resources and ultimately fail in the task they care about most: raising healthy and responsible children. Their concept is based on five key premises, as follows: (1) human energy is a precious resource that makes possible everything we wish to do; (2) energy is a *finite* quantity—there is a limited supply available to each of us; (3) *whenever the expenditure of energy exceeds the supply, burnout begins;* (4) parents who hope to accomplish the goals they have set for themselves and their children must not squander their vital resources foolishly; and (5) wasteful drains on that supply should be identified and eliminated and priority given to building the reserve.

What is it like to experience parental burnout? According to Procaccini and Kiefaber, it occurs in five progressive stages, each more stressful than the ones before. The first can be called the *"Gung ho"* stage, where parents try to do it all. It may actually begin with the discovery of pregnancy and continue for several years. Very subtly, then, parents can move from the first to the second stage of burnout, which is characterized by persistent doubts. They may know something is wrong at this point, yet fail to realize how rapidly they are losing altitude. They are frequently irritated by the children and find themselves screaming on occasion. Quite often they feel drained and fatigued. A full range of psychosomatic symptoms may come and go, including back and neck aches, upset stomach, ulcers and colitis, hypertension, headaches, diarrhea, and constipation. Still, the individual may wonder, *Why do I feel this way?* Jack, the author of the letter in the previous chapter, is a classic example of such a parent.

What will happen if Jack and his wife do not find some source of relief? Well, fortunately, their baby will not always be so demanding. But toddlerhood lies ahead, and new babies are always a possibility. If they continue to give out without taking in, they will slide from the second stage of burnout into the third.

Transition Stage

According to Procaccini and Kiefaber, this is the most critical phase. They call it the *transition stage* because decisions are usually made during this period that will determine the well-being of the family for years to come. They will either recognize the downward path they are on and make changes to reverse it, or else they will continue their plunge toward chaos.

What is felt during this third stage is indescribable fatigue, self-condemnation, great anger, and resentment. For the first time, a mother and father in this situation openly blame the kids for their discontent. One of the reasons they were so excited about parenthood was their idealistic expectation of what children are like. They honestly did not know that little boys and girls can be, and usually are, demanding, self-centered, sloppy, lazy, and rebellious. It wasn't supposed to be this way! In fact, they expected the kids to meet *their* needs for love and appreciation. Instead it is give! give! give! for the parents and take! take! take! by the children. Depression and tears are daily visitors.

The human mind will not tolerate that level of agitation for very long. It will seek to protect itself from further pain. As indicated earlier, this transition phase usually leads either to beneficial changes or to a destructive self-defense. The latter occurs in stage four, which the authors call *pulling away*. The individual withdraws from the family and becomes "unavailable" to the children. The mother may not even hear them, even though they tug at her skirt and beg for her attention. She may slip into alcoholism or drug or tranquilizer abuse to dull her senses further. If forced to deal with the minor accidents and irritants of childhood, such as spilled milk or glue on the carpet, she may overreact violently and punish wildly. Child abuse is only an inch away. It occurs thousands of times daily in most Western countries.

If asked to explain what she is feeling, a mother in the fourth stage of burnout will say something like, "I just can't deal with the kids right now." I counseled a woman in this situation who told me, referring to her children, "They hang around my ankles and beg for this or that, but I'll tell you, I kick 'em off. I'm not going to let 'em destroy my life!" She was a living, breathing stick of dynamite waiting to be ignited. People who reach this stage not only pull away from their children, but they tend to become isolated from their spouses and other family members too. Thus, being physically and psychologically exhausted, guilt-ridden to the core, drenched in self-hatred, and disappointed with life, these parents descend into the fifth stage of burnout.

The final phase is called *chronic disenchantment* by Procaccini and Kiefaber. It is characterized by confusion and apathy. The individual at this stage has lost all meaning and purpose in living. Identity is blurred. Weeks may pass with nothing of significance being remembered. Sexual desire is gone and the marriage is seriously troubled. Recurring thoughts may focus on suicide, "cracking up," or running away. Clearly, this individual is desperately in need of counseling and a radical shift in lifestyle. If nothing changes, neither generation will ever be quite the same again.

And it is all so unnecessary!

The Blur of Parenting

Now let's take a closer look at the typical home today. You may never reach the latter stages of burnout described above. Life is hard, but it isn't *that* hard. You may, however, spend your parenting years in a state of general fatigue and stress, perhaps characterized by stage two. You'll crowd your days with junk…with unnecessary responsibilities and commitments that provide no lasting benefits. Precious energy resources will be squandered on that which only *seems* important at the moment. Consequently, your parenting years will pass in a blur of irritation and frustration.

How can you know if this is happening even now? Well, continual screaming, nagging, threatening, punishing, criticizing, and scolding of children is a pretty sure tip-off. There is a better way to raise sons and daughters—and it starts with slowing down.

I know it isn't easy to implement a slower lifestyle. Prior commitments have to be met. Financial pressures must be confronted. Your employer seldom *asks* if you want to accept a new assignment. Your business would fail without your supervision. Your patients have no other physician to whom they can turn. The women's Bible study at church is counting on your leadership. There seems to be no place to stop.

Besides, isn't everyone else doing the same thing? Sure they are. Almost everyone I know is running at a breathless pace. My physician, my lawyer, my accountant, my handyman, my mechanic, my pastor, the mom down the street. There is symbolic sweat on the brow of virtually every man and woman in North America.

Most of these fathers and mothers will admit that they're too busy and working too hard, but an interesting response occurs when this subject is raised. They have convinced themselves that their overcommitment is a *temporary* problem.

> "Well, this is a difficult year, you see, because I'm going to night school and try-ing to earn a living at the same time. But it won't always be so hectic at our house. I figure I'll have my degree by a year from June. Then pressure will ease up."

or...

> "My husband and I just bought this new business, and it's gonna take us a year to get it rolling. Then we can hire the help we need. Until then, though, we're hav-ing to work ten to twelve hours a day.

That cuts into our family life quite a bit, but it won't last very long."

or...

"We just moved into a new house, and I've had to put in all the yards and build on a room in back. Every Saturday and most evenings are invested in that project. My son keeps asking me to fly a kite with him and go fishing and stuff, and I wish I could. I keep telling him if he can wait 'til next summer we'll have a lot of time to do those things."

or...

"I had a baby two weeks ago and he's not sleeping through the night, so our schedule is all haywire now. I figure it'll be kinda difficult until we get him in kindergarten."

Most people can tell you with a straight face that the pressures they feel are the result of temporary circumstances. Their future will be less hectic.

A slower day is coming. A light shines at the end of the dark tunnel.

Unfortunately, their optimism is usually unjustified. It is my observation that the hoped-for period of tranquillity rarely arrives. Instead, these short-term pressures have a way of becoming sandwiched back-to-back, so that families emerge from one crisis and sail directly into another. Thus, we live our entire lives in the fast lane, hurtling down the road toward heart failure or other catastrophic diseases. We have deluded ourselves into believing that circumstances have forced us to work too hard and take on too many activities, when, in fact, we are driven from *within*. We lack the discipline to limit our entanglements with the world, choosing instead to be dominated by our work, our materialistic desires, our hobbies, and what seem unavoidable obligations.

Just Say No

Life doesn't have to be this way. The habit of taking on too many commitments can be broken by employing one little word: No.

You may be thinking, *It's not that simple. I need that promotion to get ahead in my field...we need the extra money from my second job...I need the relaxation that comes from shopping or golfing on weekends...and what will the PTA or the church board think if I stop volunteering?*

And maybe you do need to continue with most of the activities that fill your days. No doubt there is value in each of them. But I challenge you to think for a few moments before you reply to the next request to direct the school play or accept that overtime assignment to impress the boss.

The apostle Paul wrote that we are "to say 'No' to ungodliness and worldly passions, and to live self-controlled, upright and godly lives in this present age" (Titus 2:12). Self-control starts with saying no to frantic living—and yes to a more orderly existence.

Self-control starts with saying no to frantic living—and yes to a more orderly existence.

Putting Family First

What, you may ask, does an orderly home look like? Well, it may include a mother or father who is home to greet the children in the afternoon when they return from school…a family that eats dinner together most evenings and has time to talk about their day…children who regularly help their parents with upkeep of the house through specified chores…mothers and fathers who set aside time on weekends to talk, play, and simply "be" with their kids…parents who are home in the evenings to tuck their children into bed. It may seem an idealistic picture, but almost anything is possible for those who set their minds to it.

There are encouraging signs that an increasing number of families are discovering the value of saying no and taking control of their schedules. According to a 2001 U.S. Census Bureau report, 55 percent of women with infants under a year old were in the workforce in June 2000, down from 59 percent in 1998. It represented the first decline in twenty-five years.[5]

Meanwhile, a 2000 study conducted by the Hartford Institute for Religion Research showed that 71 percent of churchgoing men reported "scaling back" at work during the previous two years to spend more time with their families.[6] This echoed the findings of a Cornell University study from the late 1990s showing that three-fourths of middle-income couples in upstate New York were reducing their work commitments for the sake of their families and to have more discretionary time.[7]

Yes, cutting back on career opportunities and other commitments is a sacrifice. But there is no harm in taking a little longer to fulfill your dreams. Remember that Satan, who once attempted to entice Jesus with the "authority and splendor" of this world (Luke 4:6), will try the same with you. He will make every effort to fill your days with temporary pleasures and treasures in order to lure you away from your family. But when you are so occupied with "important" activities that you don't have a moment for your spouse or children, it's a victory for the devil. Don't listen to him!

The first step in turning the corner is to pray over every decision that will separate you physically or emotionally from your family. Then be ready to embrace the word *no*. Energy and time are precious resources that, once lost, can never be recovered. Let's spend them in ways that create joyful, eternal memories for the loved ones under our roofs.

Doing Too Much?
Solution #2
Just Say "No" to Overcommitment

- Ask your spouse, "Are we experiencing parental burnout?" If either of you answers yes, decide what stage you are in and discuss what to do about it.

- For the next month, when someone asks you to take on a new commitment, try saying no instead of yes. At the end of the month, observe what the effect is on you and your family.

- Make a list of all of your family's current commitments; then take them to the Lord in prayer and ask if any should be removed.

Do More with Less

> *"A man's life does not consist in the*
> *abundance of his possessions."*
>
> LUKE 12:15

Would you like to know what Americans think of money and the junk it will buy? Turn on a television any weekday and watch contestants compete for prizes and cash on shows such as *Wheel of Fortune, The Price is Right,* or *Who Wants to Be a Millionaire.* Though these programs may be history by the time you read these words, there will be others to take their place. Observe the cuckoo birds as they leap in the air, frothing at the mouth and tearing at the clothes of the moderator. Notice their dilated eyes and their bright pink ears. It's an unfortunate condition known as *game show greed,* and those afflicted can find themselves squarely on the path toward burnout.

How do I know so much about game show greed? Because I've been there! Way back in 1967, my lovely wife managed to drag me to the *Let's Make a Deal* show. Shirley put toy birds all over her head and blouse, and I carried a dumb sign that said, "My wife is for the birds." Really funny, huh? It was good enough for host Monty Hall, however, and we were selected as lucky contestants. They placed us in two front seats near the cameras, but began the program by "dealing" with other suckers.

As I sat in the contestants' row, I kept thinking, *What in the world am I doing here with this stupid sign?* I couldn't have been more skeptical about the proposition. Finally, Monty called our names and we awaited the verdict.

"Here behind Door #1 is…A NEW CAR!" (the audience went crazy with excitement).

Suddenly, I was gripped by a spasm in the pit of my stomach. My mouth watered profusely and my heart began knocking on the sides of my chest. There on that stage was the car of my dreams—a brand-new Camaro. Desire came charging up my throat and stuck in the region of my Adam's apple. My breathing became irregular and shallow, which was another unmistakable clue. I had been struck by game show greed.

To understand this reaction, you would have to know that I had owned several of the worst cars in automotive history. Throughout my college years I drove a 1949 Mercury convertible that had power seats, power windows, power top, power everything…but no power to run them. I put the windows up in the winter and down in the summer. There they remained, despite fluctuating temperatures.

Shirley, who was then my girlfriend, must have loved me tremendously to have tolerated that car. She *hated* it. The front seat had a spring with a bad temper that tore her clothes and punctured her skin. Nor did Ol' Red always choose to run. Shirley spent more than one evening guiding that hunk of scrap iron slowly down the road while I pushed from behind. Talk about hurting your college pride!

The crowning blow occurred shortly after our graduation from college. We were invited to appear for important job interviews, and we put on our Sunday best for the occasion. There we were, suit and tie, heels and hose, going sixty miles an hour down the road in Ol' Red, when the top suddenly blew off. Strings and dust flapped us in the face as the canvas waved behind the car like Superman's cape. The ribs of the top protruded above our heads, reminiscent of undersized roll bars. And can you believe that Shirley got mad at *me* for letting that happen! She crouched on the floorboard of the car, criticizing me for driving such a beat-up automobile. It is a miracle that our relationship survived that emotional afternoon.

Although Ol' Red had been put to sleep long before the *Let's Make a Deal* experience, I still had never owned a new car. Every available dollar had gone to pay school bills at the University of Southern California in my pursuit of a doctorate, which was earned just two months prior to the television venture.

This explains my reaction to the beautiful automobile behind Door #1.

"All you have to do to win the car," said Monty, "is tell us the prices of these four items." Shirley and I guessed the first three, but the deck was stacked on number four. It was a Hoover portable vacuum cleaner, whose price turned out to be $53. We had to guess within $3, as I recall. We consulted each other during the commercial break and took a wild shot at $108.

"Sorry," said Monty Hall. "You've been zonked. But here, take the vacuum cleaner (wow!) and the $3 you won on the other mystery items. And thanks for playing *Let's Make a Deal.*"

On the way home, Shirley and I talked about how our emotions had been manipulated in that situation. We had both experienced incredible greed, and the feeling was not comfortable. Materialism may be the American way, but an unfettered desire for money and possessions can leave any family depleted—financially, physically, and emotionally.

An unfettered desire for possessions can leave any family depleted—financially, physically, and emotionally.

Affluenza

For many men and women, the underlying motivation behind career ambition is often that desire for more—more money to buy more things. Owning bigger and better homes and cars, the latest fashions, or the most advanced kitchen appliance or stereo system, however, will *not* bring happiness—and the time and energy spent acquiring and maintaining such possessions usually comes at the expense of the family. There is a reason why Scripture states that "the love of money is a root of all kinds of evil" (1 Timothy 6:10).

The Society of Human Resource Professionals reports that nearly 40 percent of America's labor force spends at least fifty hours a week on the job.[8] Many of these employees are fathers and mothers working overtime just to meet the monthly payments on home mortgages, car loans, and credit card debt. We are a nation of spenders—American consumers owe approximately $1.7 *trillion* in credit card and other debt.[9]

Perhaps equally alarming is another statistic reported a few years ago on a PBS television program called "Affluenza." It stated that the average American shops six hours a week while spending only forty minutes playing with his children.[10]

Do you see where this pattern leads? The desire to acquire wealth and possessions drives us to work harder and longer hours at the office, robbing us of energy and time. Even the act of going to the store and spending all our hard-earned money takes time that could have been spent relaxing with our spouse and children. It is an exhausting, vicious cycle, and it does not end at the point of purchase.

The Price of Ownership

It can accurately be said that everything you own will eventually own you. I remember experiencing the truth of this proverb when I moved into a new office some years ago. An interior designer came by and suggested that I spread a few decorator items around for effect. Among his ideas was the proposal that I buy a chime clock for the wall. The cost was nearly two hundred dollars, and I declined. But he talked to Shirley, and together they convinced me that I couldn't possibly live without that clock. So what was I to do?

The interior designer purchased the clock for me and hung it in a conspicuous spot on the wall. It functioned properly for a couple of months and then suddenly lost its mind. The chime didn't know the time of day and began gonging wildly at odd hours. Thus irritated, I dug through the files to find the guarantee. Then the clock had to be boxed and transported to the repair shop. It was retrieved five days later and hung on the wall again.

A month later, the chime went haywire once more. The entire process of repairing the clock had to be repeated. And so it went. It has now been more than twenty years since I purchased that piece of junk, and it has never worked for more than six months at a time. Over and over I have been through the "fix-it" routine. I tell you honestly that that Regulator clock hangs silently on my wall today. It still looks nice, but it no longer keeps time. I've given up on the repairman.

That wasn't the first time I regretted a purchase. I once ordered a swing set for my children identical to a shiny model I'd seen at the store. What arrived, however, was a long box containing roughly 6,324 pipes, 28,487,651 bolts, 28,487,650 screws, and a set of instructions that would have befuddled Albert Einstein. For the next two days, I sweated to assemble bent parts, missing parts, and parts from a 1948 Ford thrown in just to confuse me. Finally, the wobbly construction stood upright.

I got another shock when I read the final line

printed on the back of the instructions: "Please retighten all the bolts on this apparatus *every two weeks* to ensure safety and durability." I now had to devote every other Saturday to this tin monster or it would gobble up my children!

Do you understand what ownership of the clock and swing set cost me? I'm only allotted a specific number of days on this earth. Whatever that finite life span turns out to be, I have spent a certain percentage of those precious days in slavery to these and a thousand other gadgets. That is what material possessions do to us. To all of you boat lovers or car buffs or apartment owners out there…whatever it is that you possess…you have traded your time to buy those items, and now you must sweat to maintain them. That is the price of ownership. That is our way of life. I regret it.

Empty Castles

The folly of materialism hit home for me again during a trip to Britain years ago. As I toured the museums and historical buildings, I was struck by what I called "empty castles." Standing there in the lonely fog were edifices constructed by proud men who thought they owned them. But where are those men today? All are gone; most are forgotten. The hollow castles they left behind stand as monuments to the impermanence of man and his indifference toward what truly matters.

"Possession obsession" is a slippery slope that can lead to an avalanche. Those caught in the landslide will become less and less satisfied and will find more and more to worry about. As Solomon once wrote, "The abundance of a rich man permits him no sleep" (Ecclesiastes 5:12).

The alternative is to reject materialism, do more with less, and depend on God to meet your needs. Establish a family budget and stick within strict spending limits. Purchase items with cash whenever possible. Once you determine how much you intend to spend per month in each area, convert those amounts from your paycheck into cash and divide them into envelopes marked "food," "entertainment," and so on. When you go to the store or to the movies, use the money from the appropriate envelope. And when the envelope is empty, stop spending!

I also strongly recommend that you renew the habit of tithing if you are not already doing so.

Scripture says that "The earth is the LORD's, and everything in it" (Psalm 24:1) and "The silver is mine, and the gold is mine, saith the LORD of hosts" (Haggai 2:8, KJV). In other words, it's all God's money anyway. When you tithe, He will bless your faithfulness. I predict it will start with greater peace of mind.

I admit that it is not easy to reverse one's attitude about money and possessions, but the rewards—less stress and more time and energy for your spouse and children—are well worth it.

A. W. Tozer, a brilliant Christian theologian and author, wrote this in his outstanding book *The Pursuit of God*:

> The way to deeper knowledge of God is
> through the lonely valleys of soul poverty
> and abnegation of all things. The blessed
> ones who possess the Kingdom are they
> who have repudiated every external thing
> and have rooted from their hearts all
> sense of possessing. These are the "poor
> in spirit." They have reached an inward
> state paralleling the outward circum-
> stances of the common beggar in the

streets of Jerusalem; that is what the word "poor" as Christ used it actually means. These blessed poor are no longer slaves to the tyranny of things. They have broken the yoke of the oppressor; and this they have done not by fighting but by surrendering. Though free from all sense of possessing, they yet possess all things. "Theirs is the kingdom of heaven."[11]

We must hold all things with an open hand because, sooner or later, they will be taken from us.

Did Tozer mean by these words that it is sinful to own anything—that to follow God passionately requires us to be street people who do not possess a reliable automobile or live in a safe neighborhood? Of course not. What he is saying is that we must not let our things own us and become the central focus of our lives. We must hold all things with an open hand because, sooner or later, they will be taken from us.

Jesus said it even more graphically:

"Do not store up for yourselves treasures
on earth, where moth and rust destroy,
and where thieves break in and steal. But
store up for yourselves treasures in
heaven, where moth and rust do not
destroy, and where thieves do not break
in and steal. For where your treasure is,
there your heart will be also."

MATTHEW 6:19-21

Do Your Things Own You?

Solution #3

Let Go of the Desire to Acquire

- Are you afflicted with "possession obsession"? If so, what can you do to change it?

- If you don't already have a family budget, try writing down everything you spend for the next month. You may be surprised to see where your money is going.

- Read Matthew 19:21 and Malachi 3:8–10 in the Bible. Talk to your mate about what this means to your family.

Keeping Your Balance

This too is meaningless,
a chasing after the wind.

ECCLESIASTES 4:4

We've been talking about parents who are so focused on pursuing careers, wealth, and other personal interests that they are exhausted and disconnected from their families. Now we will examine the other end of the spectrum—parents who are equally busy and tired, but for very different reasons.

I am convinced that on the whole, mothers and fathers in North America are among the best in the world. They care passionately about their kids and will do anything to meet their needs. Yet the same qualities that enable them to succeed as parents—love, dedication, concern, involvement—sometimes lead them to unhealthy extremes.

Zealous moms and dads are determined to provide every advantage and opportunity for the next generation from the earliest days of infancy. That is where their hearts lie. That is what they care about most. Their devotion leads them to make what they consider to be small sacrifices on behalf of their children. They often discontinue all recreational, romantic, and restful activities that would take them away from home. Even long-term friends with whom they used to associate are now given lame excuses or are ignored altogether. *Everything* focuses on the children.

These parents are often unwilling to leave the kids with a babysitter for more than a few moments. Not even Mother Teresa would qualify as a guardian for an evening. They would never forgive themselves if something went wrong while they were frivolously indulging in fun or enter-

On the whole, mothers and fathers in North America are among the best in the world.

tainment. Imagine how they would feel if the announcer said over the public address system, "May I have your attention? Would Mr. or Mrs. James Johnson come to a house telephone, please? Your babysitter needs to know where the fire extinguisher is." No way! It's not worth it. They choose to stay home.

Such parents see life from a distorted perspective. Anything that might have the remotest negative influence on their kids becomes deeply disturbing to them, leading to overreaction and conflict. Insignificant childhood squabbles in the neighborhood, for example, or idle comments from church members can bring surprisingly heated responses. And Lord help the teacher or Sunday school worker who fails to deliver!

This compulsive approach to parenting can be destructive to a marriage, especially when only one parent is so inclined. If it is the mother, she may give herself totally to the children and have nothing left for her husband. He believes she has gone a little wacky with this mothering thing, and may even resent the kids for taking her away from him. She, in turn, despises his selfishness and becomes sole defender and caregiver for their children.

It is all too common for parents in this situation to find less and less time for each other. She focuses even more on the children while he pours his energy into his work. They become frustrated, irritable, and harried. They don't take walks or read the Scriptures together, or do anything that is fun. Their sex life suffers because exhausted people don't make love meaningfully. They begin to drift apart and eventually find themselves with "irreconcilable differences." It is a tragic pattern that I have observed often.

Burned-Out Kids

Compulsive parenting can be equally hazardous to the object of all this attention: the child. Many parents today burn out their kids with too many scheduled activities. Like Martha (Luke 10:40), they allow busyness to distract their family from what is truly important. These dedicated moms and dads want their children to experience everything that's available—motivated in part so that their kids will be able to compete with their peers when college scholarships are handed out.

Those are laudable intentions. But are all the

sports practices, singing lessons, and dance recitals worth the price? According to recent studies, America's children spend twenty-nine hours per week at school, up from twenty-one hours in 1981. Participation in organized sports has nearly doubled during the same period.[12] Free time for children, on the other hand, is down to only six hours a week.[13]

For some kids it is just too much. For example, *Newsweek* magazine reported that Andrea Galambos, a sixteen-year-old junior at a Connecticut high school, was captain of her volleyball team, first-chair flute in the school orchestra, a top player on the tennis team, and an honors student with three hours of homework a night. She also took singing and acting classes after school. As Andrea put it, "I never had more than five minutes to sit down and breathe." Andrea finally decided to continue with school and tennis and drop everything else. The change, she said, left her "totally relieved."[14]

Some parents are fighting these trends by setting definite limits on the number of activities their children can participate in. While raising their six kids, FamilyLife founders Dennis and Barbara Rainey had a rule that their sons and daughters could be involved in only one activity at a time. It helped them manage a schedule that could easily have spun out of control, exhausting them and their children.

The tendency toward overloading kids' schedules often begins early in childhood. I am especially concerned about the large quantities of homework that are routinely given during elementary school. Little kids are asked to sit for six or more hours a day doing formal classwork. Then they take that tiring bus ride home, and guess what? They're placed at a desk and told to do more assignments. For a wiry, hyperactive child or even for a fun-loving youngster, that is asking too much. Learning for them becomes an enormous bore instead of the exciting panorama that it should be.

When our kids were young, Shirley and I also found that we were trying to do many things with the limited time we had together. I wanted our kids to participate in church activities, have some family time, and still be able to kick back and waste an hour or two. Children need opportunities for unstructured play—swinging on the swings and throwing rocks and playing with a basketball. Yet by the time the homework was done, darkness had fallen and dinnertime had arrived. Then baths were taken and off they went to bed. Something didn't feel right about that kind of pace. That's why I negotiated with our children's teachers, agreeing that the kids would complete no more than one hour per night of supervised homework. It was enough!

Superparenting

If I have been describing you and your family in these harried examples, please understand that I am not critical of the motives behind what might be called "superparenting." Children *are* worth our very best efforts to raise them properly, and I have spent the majority of my life urging parents to give them their due. Nevertheless, even a noble and necessary task can be taken to such extremes that it becomes harmful to both the giver and the receiver. For moms and dads, obsessive child-rearing can eventually lead to dangerous levels of exhaustion. In the child's case, there is a direct link between superparenting and overprotection, an egocentric perspective on life, and in some cases, a prolonged dependency relationship with parents.

Obsessive child-rearing can eventually lead to dangerous levels of exhaustion.

Superparenting is a natural trap for those of us who share the Christian faith. Deeply ingrained within us is a philosophy that lends itself to compulsive child-rearing. The family ranks near the top of our value system, and our way of life focuses on self-sacrifice and commitment to others. Does it not seem reasonable, therefore, that we would pour every resource into this awesome task? That is our God-given assignment, isn't it?

Well, of course it is, but I would point out that the apostle Paul advocates "moderation" in all things (Philippians 4:5, KJV). *Balance* is the key to successful living…and parenting.

A Time to Give, a Time to Escape

I have already admitted that I have struggled at times to achieve a proper perspective between my profession and my family. This inclination to over-schedule was particularly prevalent during the first decade of my marriage. Gradually, however, Shirley and I came to understand that the Lord wanted us to use good judgment and common sense in the things we agreed to do and the activities we involved our children in. There will always be more worthwhile things to do than a family can get done. We realized that we needed to maintain a healthy balance between Christian duty, work responsibilities, recreation, social obligations, and meaningful family life.

I came across two Scripture references that helped clarify this issue. The first is found in Matthew 14:13–14: "When Jesus heard what had happened [to John the Baptist], he withdrew by boat privately to a solitary place. Hearing of this, the crowds followed him on foot from the towns. When Jesus landed and saw a large crowd, he had compassion on them and healed their sick."

Jesus was undoubtedly grieving at that time over the beheading of His cousin and friend, John the Baptist. He needed to withdraw "privately to a solitary place." Nevertheless, the people learned of His whereabouts and came seeking His healing touch. Even in that painful time of loss, Jesus took compassion on the people and reached out to those in need. From this I concluded that there are times when we, too, must give of ourselves even when it is difficult or inconvenient to do so.

But there was another occasion when thousands of people sought to be healed by Jesus. After spending some time with them, He got in a boat with His disciples and rowed away. Mark 4:36 says, "Leaving the crowd behind, they took [Jesus] along, just as he was, in the boat." Undoubtedly, the large following that day included individuals with cancer, blindness, physical deformities, and every other kind of human misery. Jesus could have stayed there through the night and healed them all, yet He had apparently reached the end of His strength and knew He needed to rest.

A similar event is described in Matthew 14:23, where we read, "And when he had sent the multitudes away, he went up into a mountain apart to pray: and when the evening was come, he was there alone" (KJV).

Just as there is a time to give, there is also a time to be alone, to pray and escape from the pressures of the day—even though there are worthy things yet to be accomplished. Those who fail to reserve some downtime for rest and renewal—as

Jesus did—are risking even the good things they want to accomplish. That is true for parents *and* for their children.

I once read an article in the *Los Angeles Times* about a man named J. R. Buffington. His goal in life was to produce lemons of record-breaking size from the tree in his backyard. He came up with a formula to do just that. He fertilized the tree with ashes from the fireplace, some rabbit and goat manure, a few rusty nails, and plenty of water. That spring, the scrawny little tree produced two gigantic lemons, one weighing over five pounds. But every other lemon on the tree was shriveled and misshapen. Mr. Buffington is still working on his formula.

Isn't that the way it is in life? Great investments in a particular endeavor tend to rob others of their potential. I'd rather have a tree covered with juicy lemons than a record-breaking but freakish crop, wouldn't you? *Balance* is the word. As parents, we must appropriately divide our time and energy between family and other activities while pausing regularly to refresh. Then we must help our sons and daughters do the same.

Solution #4

Seek Balance for Your Life and Family

- Talk with your family—are your lives more like a normal lemon tree or like J. R. Buffington's? How might you achieve balance at home?

- If you tend to be so focused on your children that your marriage is suffering, gently ask for your partner's forgiveness. Talk together about ways to maintain your devotion to your kids while increasing your attention on your mate.

- Look at your schedule for the next week. If it is so full that you have no time to rest and refresh, see what you can rearrange to provide for an "escape."

Turn Off, Tune In

The wisdom of this world is foolishness
in God's sight.

1 CORINTHIANS 3:19

David, a man in his thirties, is not a fan of television. I will let him explain why.

"In many ways I feel that I was deprived of parents because of the invention of TV..." David says. "When I was growing up, their attention was *always* on the TV. I could speak to them only during the commercials. I can still hear my mom's voice say, 'Not now. The show's started—wait until the commercials.' Other times Dad would bark, 'Can't you see we're trying to watch TV?'"

David now lives in Japan. When he returned home recently to visit his parents, he noticed that little had changed.

"They sat there mesmerized by the television," David said. "I felt they saw me as a distraction to their TV routine. I'm amazed how they chose to miss out on real interaction with their son, whom they don't see often, in favor of the television."[15]

Unfortunately, the picture that David paints of his parents is a common one. In fact, with the proliferation of the use of computers, the Internet, video games, and DVDs and videos, the time that all members of the family spend in front of video screens of one type or another has never been greater.

How much time are we talking about? According to *Business Week* magazine, Americans average nine and a half hours each day watching television, going to movies, renting videos, reading magazines, listening to music, or surfing the Internet.[16] Incredibly, that is a total of sixty-six and a half hours of media consumption per week! Assuming that we sleep eight hours each night, these data shows that nearly 60 percent of our waking hours are devoted to these passive providers of entertainment, communication, and information.

Nearly **60** percent of our **waking** hours are devoted to these **passive** providers of **entertainment,** communication, and information.

It is a family addiction. Teenagers between thirteen and seventeen watch four hours of television a day on weekdays.[17] The habit even extends to preschoolers—children ranging in age from six months to six years devote about two hours per day to watching television, playing video games, or using computers. That's roughly the same amount of time they spend playing outdoors and three times as long as they spend reading or being read to.[18]

These are alarming trends. As a nation, we are allocating enormous amounts of a precious resource—our time—to activities that often provide little benefit other than a temporary diversion from the problems of the day. It's no wonder that we have so little time to get it all done—we spend the majority of our days sitting in a chair staring at a TV or computer screen.

This obsession has allowed the media to dictate our schedules and isolate us from one another. It is a primary reason for the breakdown of families today. Husbands and wives have no time for each other, and many of them hardly know their children. Even when we do take time to be with our loved ones, it is often so crowded with multiple tasks that the experience is more hurried than healthy.

Pollster George Barna has observed this trend with teens. He wrote, "It is becoming less common these days for a teenager to have time isolated for focused interaction with family members. Most of the time they spend with their family is what you might call 'family and time': family and TV, family and dinner, family and homework, etc. The lives of each family member are usually so jam-packed that the opportunity to spend time together doing unique activities— talking about life, visiting special places, playing games, and sharing spiritual explorations—has to be scheduled in advance. Few do so."[19]

It takes time to build a relationship, whether it is with a best friend, your spouse, or your son or daughter. The moments you'll cherish most occur

not during a scheduled activity, but in the free-
dom of unstructured and unpressured time
together.

The author of Hebrews wrote, "Let us not
give up meeting together, as some are in the habit
of doing" (Hebrews 10:25). He was speaking
specifically about fellowship with believers, but it
applies just as much to fellowship with friends
and family. This is what we lose when we spend
hour after hour glued to the television or computer.

In addition, when parents are involved intimately with their kids during the teen years and
when their relationship leads to an active family
life, rebellious and destructive behavior is less
likely to occur. Dr. Blake Bowden and colleagues
at Cincinnati Children's Hospital studied 527
teenagers to learn what family and lifestyle charac-
teristics were related to mental health and
adjustment. The findings were significant.

Adolescents whose parents ate dinner with
them five times per week or more were the least
likely to be on drugs, be depressed, or be in
trouble with the law. They were more likely to be
doing well in school and to be surrounded by a
supportive circle of friends. By contrast, the

poorly adjusted teens ate with their parents only three evenings per week or less. What Bowden's study shows is that children do far better in school and in life when they spend time with their parents, and specifically, when they get together almost every day for conversation and interaction.[20]

MTV Madness

The media does more than steal our time, of course. The harmful effects of watching contemporary television, movies, and video games are well documented. One of the most conclusive studies was conducted years ago by Dr. Leonard D. Aaron. He examined a group of children from the United States, Australia, and Finland at age eight, again at nineteen, and once more at thirty. The outcome was the same; the more frequently the participants watched violent television at age eight, the more likely they were to be convicted of crimes by age thirty, and the more aggressive was their behavior when drinking.[21] Similarly, two recent studies found that exposure to violent video games increased aggressive behavior in both the short and long term.[22]

Today's popular music also frequently has a negative impact on impressionable listeners. Rock stars are the heroes, the idols, that young people want to emulate. When these role models are depicted in violent and sexual roles, many teenagers and preadolescents are pulled along in their wake.

What could possibly be wholesome about showing explicit sexual scenes—especially those involving perversions—to twelve- and thirteen-year-old kids? Yet music videos come into the home via MTV and other channels that feature men and women in blatantly sexual situations, or even in depictions of sadism. One of MTV's "stars" was recently shown being sloshed around upside down in a portable toilet; he ate a live goldfish and then vomited it into a bowl. A steady diet of this garbage will pollute the minds of even the healthiest of teenagers.

If a complete stranger came to your door and said, "You look tired. Why don't you let me take care of your children for a day or two?" I doubt that you would say, "Great idea. Come on in." Yet that is essentially what thousands of parents do when they allow their children unlimited and unmonitored access to television, movies, video games, the Internet, music CDs, and DVDs. It is an increasingly dangerous thing to do.

Ending Media Mania

How, then, should we respond to these seemingly innocent "strangers" who not only steal our valuable time but also attempt to alter the values of our family? Is it even possible to influence our environment in today's "anything goes" culture?

The answer is yes. There *are* solutions. But they require employing one of the fruits of the Spirit described by the apostle Paul: self-control (Galatians 5:23).

If your family is dominated by media mania, you can change the pattern by establishing a system that sets reasonable limits on your family's media consumption. Regarding the television, for example, you might first sit down with your children and agree upon a list of approved programs that are appropriate for each age level. Then type or write that list and enclose it in clear plastic so it can be referred to throughout the week.

Second, either purchase or make a roll of tickets. Issue each child ten tickets per week, and let him or her use them to "buy" the privilege of watching the programs on the approved list. When the tickets are gone, television viewing is over for that week. This teaches a child to be discriminating about what is watched. A maximum of ten hours of viewing per week might be an appropriate place to start, depending on age.

This system can also be applied to playing video games, surfing the Internet, or listening to music. The idea is to put definite limits on the minutes or hours your children spend with the media, restricting its influence and creating more time for the rest of their lives.

The real test, of course, is whether you as the parent have the courage and persistence to put yourself on the same system. If you do, you'll set a proper example for your family *and* discover time you never realized you had to relax, accomplish what needs to be done, and enjoy being with your children.

Another approach is an experiment recommended by Bob DeMoss, author of *TV: The Great Escape*. DeMoss advises his readers to break bad habits by disconnecting their televisions for thirty days. Here are a few comments from parents who tried it:

> "The greatest gift to me of having the TV off has been the gift of time. Time for the kids to have a leisurely snack after school and then do homework instead of working to cram it in before or after favorite TV programs. Time created by sleeping more and therefore making my waking hours more productive. Time to savor and make the most of the final weeks of summer. Time for our kids to play with each other. Time for their imaginations to take hold and creatively express themselves."
>
> Debbie, Austin, Texas

> "Sent out a bunch of letters today. I really love writing. People have asked recently where I've found the time...I've really noticed how much I get done in the morning now that I'm not vegging in front of the boob tube."
>
> Jennifer, Pottstown, Pennsylvania

"I will not allow TV back in my home…I have no idea how I would get anything done if I had TV at home again."

   Kimberly, Sharon Hill, Pennsylvania[23]

Even those parents who went back to watching TV after participating in the thirty-day challenge found that television no longer had a stranglehold on their lives—they turned it on less often and found it easier to turn off objectionable programming. This experiment can be applied to any form of media that is wreaking havoc in your home.

Pulling the Plug—Permanently

A more straightforward solution for obsessive viewing and listening habits was described to me years ago in this letter from a discerning little girl named Tanya:

Dear Sir:
   In your last Newsletter you asked me to help support your television

project. I'm writing to let you know why I won't. First, we don't even have a T.V. Second, we send our extra money to Missionaries. Third, I'm only eleven years old and I don't have any money.

Now I want to go back to the first reason, because it is the most important one. In Psalm 101:3 it says: "I will set no wicked thing before my eyes." I have never lived with a television. My parents never bought one. But from reading and hearing other people talk, I understand there are people shown on television who don't have enough clothes on. People who steal, kill, lie and cheat and swear. My parents have taught me, and the Bible says, those things are wicked.

Maybe this doesn't make sense to you, but it does to me. I don't think I'm missing anything, because we get to travel a lot and read lots and lots of books.

Yours truly,
Tanya

As I wrote to Tanya then, her letter made plenty of sense to me. It is those of us who devote hours each day to absorbing misguided forms of "entertainment" who are missing something! I respect Tanya and her family for having the courage not to own a set. You too may decide that getting rid of the television or computer is the right choice for you and your family.

A New Kind of Music

Simon Verity is a master stone carver who honed his craft restoring thirteenth-century cathedrals in Great Britain. With each careful blow of his chisel, Verity listened closely to the song of the stone. A solid strike indicated that all was well. But a higher-pitched *ping* meant that a chunk of rock might be ready to break off. He constantly adjusted the angle of his blows and the force of his mallet to the pitch, pausing frequently to run his hand over the freshly carved surface. Verity's success depended on his ability to read the signals being sung by his stones.

In a similar way, when you clear away the distractions that invade your home through devices such as television and the computer, you also will begin to hear the "music" of your spouse and children. Time that was once spent in front of the "idiot box" can instead be devoted to conversation, playing games, taking walks, and simply listening to each other.

As you turn off electronic distractions and tune in to your family, you will also find it easier to discern the quiet, still voice of our Lord. More time in your schedule can lead to a richer prayer life, deeper understanding of His Word, and fulfillment of the words of the psalmist: "May all who seek you rejoice and be glad in you" (Psalm 40:16).

In a finite life where every moment counts, these may be the greatest benefits of all.

Solution #5

Turn Off Distractions and Tune In to Your Loved Ones

- How much time do you think each member of your family spends watching television or movies, surfing the Internet, or playing video games? For a week, have everyone in the family record the time they spend on each of these activities; then compare it to your estimate.

- Talk it over with your family, and then try Bob DeMoss's suggestion to disconnect your TV for a month—or even a week. At the end of the experiment, make a list of advantages and disadvantages you discovered.

- I strongly urge you to remove television sets, computers, video games, VCRs, and DVD players from your kids' bedrooms. Locate them in the family room, where they can be monitored and where the amount of time spent on them is regulated. How can you do less for your children?

Encouragement for Today

*Encourage one another and
build each other up.*

1 THESSALONIANS 5:11

I f we don't protect ourselves from outside stresses, life can seem more like a marathon than a stroll in the park. With relentless pressure at work, a demanding schedule of carpooling and sports, and the stress of keeping up with home and church duties, moms and dads can begin to lose heart. Then fatigue and irritability set in, angry words are spoken, and soon every member of the family is at one another's throats.

Each of us wields great power to build up—or tear down—those around us. Lewis Yablonsky, author of *Fathers and Sons,* wrote about the effect of negative comments on his own father. At the dinner table, Lewis's mother would say things like, "Look at your father! His shoulders are bent down; he's a failure. He doesn't have the courage to get a better job or make more money. He's a beaten man." Yablonsky's father never defended himself. He just kept staring at his plate.

Compare this story with that of one of literature's most famous names, Nathaniel Hawthorne, and his wife. Sophia Hawthorne secretly set aside a few dollars each week, a savings that eventually grew large enough to support them both for a year. You see, Sophia believed that her husband would one day be a great writer. When Hawthorne came home one day and announced in disgrace that he'd been fired from his job in a customhouse, Sophia presented him with the money, saying, "Now you can write your book!" Her confidence and encouragement led to one of America's classic novels, *The Scarlet Letter*.

A kind word. . .fuels our energy and infuses us with new enthusiasm for facing the challenges life throws our way.

Mark Twain once said, "I can live for two months on a good compliment." A kind word is like that. It fuels our energy and infuses us with new enthusiasm for facing the challenges life throws our way. One of the best solutions for couples battling parental burnout is a simple one: Apply the words of Scripture and "encourage one another daily, as long as it is called Today" (Hebrews 3:13).

Help for the Harried Wife

We have already touched on the common problem of husbands (or wives) who commit enormous amounts of time and energy to their careers or any other intense interest. They often exhaust themselves and may leave virtually all home and parenting duties to their equally drained spouses. Both parents will eventually burn out, and their children and marriages will suffer accordingly.

This career-minded or otherwise-occupied spouse, most often the husband, is physically and emotionally "elsewhere." The wife, meanwhile, is often left isolated and alone. It is likely that she has no extended family to rely on. She may pass two or four or even ten years without a significant break from the tasks of child-rearing. She feels it is a minor sacrifice to make for so great a purpose. The impact on her psychologically, however, may be devastating. Women, especially, tend to derive their sense of self-worth from the emotional closeness achieved through relationships.

Husbands, it is time you realized that your wives are under attack. Hardly a day passes when the traditional values of the Judeo-Christian heritage are not blatantly mocked and undermined:

- The notion that motherhood is a worthwhile investment of a woman's time suffers unrelenting bombardment.
- The idea that wives should yield to the leadership of their husbands, as commanded in Ephesians 5:21–33, is considered almost medieval in its stupidity.
- The concept that a man and woman should become one flesh, finding their identity in each other rather than as separate and competing individuals, is said to be intolerably insulting to women.

- The belief that divorce is an unacceptable alternative has been abandoned by practically everybody.
- The description of the ideal wife and mother as offered in Proverbs 31:10–31 is now unthinkable for the modern woman.
- The role of the female as helpmeet, bread baker, wound patcher, love giver, home builder, and child bearer is seen as nothing short of disgusting.

All of these deeply ingrained values, which many wives are trying desperately to sustain, are exposed to continuing ridicule. The Western media—radio, television, and the press—are working relentlessly to shred the last vestiges of Christian tradition. And wives who believe in that spiritual heritage are virtually hanging by their thumbs! They are made to feel stupid, old-fashioned, and unfulfilled, and in many cases, their self-esteem is suffering irreparable damage. They are fighting more than three decades of social change with very little support from anyone.

Let me say it more directly. For the man who appreciates the willingness of his wife to stand against the tide of public opinion—staying at home in her empty neighborhood in the exclusive company of jelly-faced toddlers and strong-willed adolescents—it is about time you gave her some help. I'm not merely suggesting that you wash the dishes or sweep the floor. I'm referring to the provision of emotional support…of conversation…of making her feel like a lady…of building her ego…of giving her one day of recreation each week…of taking her out to dinner…of telling her that you love her. Without these armaments, she is left weary and defenseless against the foes of the family—the foes of *your* family!

Jesus gave us a classic example of this kind of unselfish service when He washed His disciples' feet and told them to do the same for one another. Is it time for some symbolic "foot washing" in your marriage? Women are romantic creatures. God made them that way. Have you tried to understand that tender nature and sought to meet the needs it expresses?

Is it time for some symbolic "foot washing" in your marriage?

I also must point out that even if you do lavish attention on your wife, you still will not be able to meet all of her emotional needs. Encourage her to develop meaningful friendships with other women and to reach out to others in your community. Perhaps she can join a church Bible study or a Mothers of Preschoolers (MOPS) group. Even a few refreshing breaks in the routine can lift her spirits for days to come.

Appreciating Your Husband

There are two sides to every coin, and it's time now that we flipped this one over. Wives, do you understand the needs of your husbands? Let's face it, a man's career is usually extremely important to his self-esteem. He is made that way. Many women complain about their husbands' "workaholism," which may be valid, and yet husbands deserve thanks for the effort they invest. Compared to the man who sits around the house doing little or nothing, the hard worker is an honorable man. God has assigned two key tasks to men: to provide for and to protect their families. If your husband meets those two requirements, you need to let him know that you appreciate how hard he works.

He will also appreciate a peaceful environment. Several years ago, a survey was taken to determine what men wanted in their homes. The result was surprising: It was *tranquillity*. Is your home a haven for your husband and family—a place where he can "recharge his batteries" and enjoy the company of his loved ones?

One last point for wives to remember—your man needs your *respect*. Compliment him on the qualities you most admire in him. Avoid comments that debase or embarrass him, especially in the eyes of others. As much as is reasonably possible, understand and support his career, but also create such an affirming atmosphere at home that he will be happy to leave career concerns at the office.

Barnabas, whose name means "son of encouragement," was "full of the Holy Spirit and faith" (Acts 11:24). His gift was invaluable in helping the apostle Paul lead others to Christ during their missionary journeys. If you are willing to be a Barnabas to your spouse and seek the Lord's help, He will bless you with renewed strength to encourage your mate.

Going It Alone

Though the task of child-rearing is truly daunting for the overworked and underappreciated mom or dad, the most likely candidate of all for burnout is the single parent. He or she deserves our sincere admiration. These individuals, usually women, must complete the duties ordinarily assigned to husbands and wives without the support and love of a partner. Their lives run not on level ground, but uphill, seven days a week.

Occasionally I meet a man or woman whose journey seems almost unbearable. I will never forget the telephone conversation I had with a young mother some years ago. We were broadcasting live on the radio, and I was attempting to answer questions of callers who sought my advice. The soft, feminine voice of a girl, perhaps twenty-three years of age, still echoes in my mind.

She was the mother of two preschool children, the youngest being a thirteen-month-old son with cerebral palsy. He could neither talk nor walk nor respond in the manner of other children his age. The older brother, then three years of age, apparently resented the attention given the baby and constantly tested the limits of his mother's authority. As we conversed, however, I learned of additional difficulties. Her husband had been unable to withstand these pressures and had departed a few months earlier. So there was this young woman, burdened by the guilt and trials of a sick baby and a rebellious toddler, also confronted by abandonment and rejection from her husband. My heart ached for her.

After broadcasting this conversation, we received dozens of letters from listeners who wanted to contact her and offer financial aid. But I couldn't help them. I only knew her as a voice— a voice that conveyed sadness and pain and fear and courage and faith.

If you are a single mother or father, I sympathize with your plight and urge you to seek help and encouragement from family, neighbors, other friends, and church. You need the friendship of two-parent families who can take your children on occasion to free up some time. If you are a mom, you need the assistance of young men who will play catch with your boys and take them to the school soccer game. You need friends who will fix the brakes on the Chevy and patch the leaky roof. You need prayer partners who will hold you accountable in your walk with the Lord and help bear your burdens. You need an extended family of believers to care for you, lift you up, and remind you of your priorities.

Perhaps most important, you need to know that the Lord is mindful of your circumstances. Remember the words of the psalmist: "You hear, O LORD, the desire of the afflicted; you encourage them, and you listen to their cry" (Psalm 10:17).

The rest of us, meanwhile, must bear in mind the scriptural command to "look after orphans and widows in their distress" (James 1:27). If you know of a burned-out single mom or dad, why not offer a helping hand? A little kindness may be just what he or she needs to make it through the day.

You need to know that the Lord is mindful of your circumstances.

Yoked Side by Side

The Greek translation for the word *encouragement* is *parakletos,* which literally means "called alongside to help." It brings to mind the biblical image of two people yoked side by side, as when Jesus said, "Take my yoke upon you and learn from me.... For my yoke is easy and my burden is light" (Matthew 11:29–30). This kind of encouragement includes offering an uplifting word, but it is more than that. It is standing by your husband and keeping an attitude of good cheer when he is laid off from his job. It is taking the kids for a Saturday when your wife is too tired to even stand. It's rearranging or postponing your plans— or even your career aspirations—when your mate is disheartened and needs your support.

Let's apply this concept, now, to you and me. What should a woman do for a man that will relate directly to his masculine nature? In a word, she can build his confidence. This vital role is best illustrated by one of my favorite stories, as it was told by my late friend Dr. E. V. Hill. E. V. was a dynamic black minister and the senior pastor of Mt. Zion Missionary Baptist Church in Los Angeles. He had lost his precious wife, Jane, to cancer. In one of the most moving messages I've ever heard, Dr. Hill spoke about Jane at her funeral and described the ways this "classy lady" made him a better man.

As a struggling young preacher, E. V. had

trouble earning a living. That led him to invest the family's scarce resources, over Jane's objections, in the purchase of a service station. She felt her husband lacked the time and expertise to oversee his investment, which proved to be accurate. Eventually, the station went broke and E. V. lost his shirt in the deal.

It was a critical time in the life of this young man. He had failed at something important, and his wife would have been justified in saying, "I told you so." But Jane had an intuitive understanding of her husband's vulnerability. Thus, when E. V. called her to tell her that he had lost the station, she simply said, "All right." E. V. came home that night expecting his wife to be pouting over his foolish investment. Instead, she sat down with him and said, "I've been doing some figuring. I figure that you don't smoke, and you don't drink. If you smoked and drank, you would have lost as much as you lost in the service station. So six in the one hand, and a half-dozen in the other. Let's forget it."

Jane could have shattered her husband's confidence at that delicate juncture. The male ego is surprisingly fragile, especially during times of failure and embarrassment. That's why E. V. needed to hear her say, "I still believe in you," and that is precisely the message she conveyed to him.

Shortly after the fiasco with the service station, E. V. came home one night and found the house dark. When he opened the door, he saw that Jane had prepared a candlelight dinner for two. "What meaneth thou this?" he said, with characteristic humor. "Well," said Jane, "we're going to eat by candlelight tonight." E. V. thought that was a great idea, and he went into the bathroom to wash his hands. He tried unsuccessfully to turn on the light. Then he felt his way to the bedroom and flipped another switch. Darkness prevailed. The young pastor went back to the dining room and asked Jane why the electricity was off.

She began to cry. "You work so hard, and we're trying," said Jane, "but it's pretty rough. I didn't have quite enough money to pay the light bill. I didn't want you to know about it, so I thought we would just eat by candlelight."

Dr. Hill described his wife's words with intense emotion. He said, "She could have said, 'I've never been in this situation before. I was reared in the home of Dr. Carruthers, and we never had our lights cut off.' She could have broken my spirit. She could have ruined me. She could have demoralized me. But instead, she said, 'Somehow or another, we'll get these lights on, but let's eat tonight by candlelight.'"

E. V. continued. "She was my protector. Some years ago I received quite a few death threats, and one night I received notice that I would be killed the next day. I woke up thankful to be alive, but I noticed that she was gone. I looked out the window, and my car was gone. I went outside, and I finally saw her driving up in her robe. I said, 'Where have you been?' She said, 'I…I…it occurred to me that they could have put a bomb in that car last night, and if you had gotten in there, you would have been blown away, so I got up and drove it. It's all right.'"

Jane Hill must have been an incredible lady. Of her many gifts and attributes, I'm most impressed by her awareness of the role she played in strengthening and supporting her husband. E. V. was a powerful Christian leader. Who would have believed that he needed his wife to build and preserve his confidence? But that's the way men are made. Most of us are a little shaky inside, especially during early adulthood.

It was certainly true for me. Shirley has contributed immeasurably to my development as a man. I've said many times that she believed in me before I believed in myself and that her respect gave me the confidence with which to compete and strive and risk. Most of what I'm doing today can be traced to the love of this devoted woman, who stood by me, saying, "I'm glad to be on your team."

What I'm trying to say is that the sexes are designed with highly specific but quite different psychological needs. Each is vulnerable to the other in unique ways. When reduced to basics, women need men to be romantic, caring, and loving, and men need women to be respectful, supportive, and loyal. These are not primarily cultural influences that are learned in childhood, as some would have us believe. They are deeply rooted forces in the human personality. Indeed, the Creator observed Adam's loneliness in the Garden of Eden and said, "It's not good for the man to be alone." So He made him a helpmate, a partner, a lover—an *encourager* designed to link with him emotionally and sexually. In so doing, he invented the family, and gave it His blessing and ordination.

Encouragement is a participation game. When you stand alongside your partner and share his or her troubles, you've become a practitioner of *parakletos* and an exceptional source of courage and hope.

Depressed? Discouraged?

Solution #6
Lift Up One Another

- Does your family practice an attitude of *parakletos*? If not, how could you move in that direction?

- Tell your spouse two ways that he or she can encourage you this week. Ask what you can do to be an encourager.

- Read examples of the way that Jesus affirmed others (Matthew 16:17–19; 26:6–13; Luke 7:44–48; and John 1:47–48).

Prayer: The Right Response

*[The LORD] gives strength to the weary and
increases the power of the weak.*

ISAIAH 40:29

Nearly three millennia ago, the prophet Elijah
achieved a great triumph over Ahab and the
prophets of Baal on Mount Carmel. God
answered Elijah's cry with a holy fire. But then
Jezebel promised to kill Elijah, so he fled into the
desert. Thoroughly drained in body and soul,
Elijah was so disheartened that he was ready to
die. He sat down and prayed, "'I have had
enough, LORD,' he said. 'Take my life'" (1 Kings
19:4).

Don't we as parents often feel just as Elijah
did? If your energy is totally depleted, if you're ill
and have nothing left to give to needy children, if

obstacles seem to thwart your every move—aren't these the moments when you too have had enough? Perhaps you have been so disheartened that you even wished for your very life to end.

So often, when we reach the end of our frazzled ropes, we keep our despair to ourselves. We try to muddle through on our own strength and eventually collapse. But Elijah, even in his great despondency, knew the right response. He took his feelings of hopelessness to the Lord in prayer. And God heard Elijah. He sent His tender answer through an angel: "The journey is too much for you" (v. 7). After sleeping, Elijah found that a meal had been prepared for him. He ate and drank, receiving new hope and strength to continue.

A **commitment** to the Lord and His ways is the foundation for life and marriage.

When overloaded schedules and unexpected demands threaten to overwhelm us, it is tempting to forgo our commitment to prayer. Yet a commitment to the Lord and His ways is the foundation for life and marriage, and a meaning-ful prayer life is essential to maintaining that commitment. It is precisely during busy times of stress and despair that we, like Elijah, most need to fall to our knees before Him.

No Appointment Needed

Can you imagine taking a spur-of-the-moment trip to the White House and immediately being ushered into the Oval Office to meet the president?

Of course you can't. You would need an appointment first—and a very good reason for being there! Yet, amazingly, you can "drop in" on someone far more important than the president of the United States. And you can expect that He will push aside all other business to talk with you.

The King of the universe—the Creator of all heaven and earth, who has no needs or shortcom-ings—loves you and me so much that He is always ready to spend time with us. That is almost incomprehensible. The Lord wants to hear about your struggles and successes, encour-age you, and share His glorious plans for you.

Prayer is a wonderful privilege—a chance for direct communication with our Creator. No matter how busy He may be, He always has time in His schedule for you.

If our almighty Father in heaven longs this much to fellowship with us, shouldn't we be willing to make prayer a priority, regardless of how busy we are? Jesus told the disciples that they "should always pray and not give up" (Luke 18:1). Christ understood better than anyone the significance of consistent prayer. No matter how exhausted and burned out we may be, we must heed the wisdom of our Savior.

I recall one night years ago when Shirley and I were particularly tired. Though we had covenanted between us to pray for our son and daughter at the close of each day, on this evening we were so exhausted that we collapsed into bed without our usual benediction. We were almost asleep when Shirley's voice pierced the night. "Jim," she said, "we haven't prayed for our kids yet today. Don't you think we should talk to the Lord?"

I admit that it was very difficult for me to pull my six-foot-two-inch frame out of our warm bed that night. Nevertheless, we got on our knees and offered a prayer for our children's safety, placing them in the hands of the Father once more.

Later we learned that Danae and a girlfriend had gone to a fast-food establishment and bought hamburgers and Cokes. They had driven up the road a few miles and were sitting in the car eating the meal when a city policeman drove by, shining his spotlight in all directions. He was obviously looking for someone, but gradually went past.

A few minutes later, Danae and her friend heard a *clunk* from under the car. They looked at one another nervously and felt a sharp bump. Before they could leave, a man crawled out from under the car and emerged on the passenger side. He was very hairy and looked like he had been on the street for weeks. The man immediately came to the door and attempted to open it. Thank God, it was locked. Danae quickly started the car and drove off…no doubt at record speed.

When we checked the timing of this incident, we realized that Shirley and I had been on our knees at the precise moment of danger. Our prayers were answered. Our daughter and her friend were safe!

It is impossible for me to overstate the need for prayer, *especially* when we think we lack the time or energy to do so. It was the apostle Paul who said, "Pray continually; give thanks in all circumstances, for this is God's will for you in Christ Jesus" (1 Thessalonians 5:17–18). As you pray continually, you will discover that the advantages of a vibrant prayer life are too vital to be ignored.

A Heavenly Relationship

The Bible places great emphasis on prayer. We read many examples of how important prayer was to Jesus (Luke 5:16). We are taught that prayer is not designed for gaining favor in the eyes of men (Matthew 6:5–6) and that we need not use "many words" in an attempt to impress Him (v. 7). We are even given examples of the words we should use (vv. 9–13).

But why, exactly, is prayer so important to our Lord? Incredibly, it is an expression of His desire to have a *relationship* with us. Though it is impossible to explain why, our Lord wishes to know us intimately—to have a personal, two-way conversation with each of His children. Though He can read our minds, He wants us to seek Him, to love

Him, and to talk with Him daily. The reason is that there is no relationship in eavesdropping!

As a father or mother, you naturally desire a close relationship with your kids. You appreciate hearing about their new discoveries and joys. And when they tell you they are overwhelmed or afraid, you quickly offer reassurance. Our heavenly Father, who loves us even more than we love our own children, responds to our prayers in the same way. If we consistently communicate with our Lord, we will find our hearts bound ever closer to Him. We'll discover the "solid rock" we need to help us withstand the daily stresses and storms of life.

If we consistently communicate with our Lord, we will find our hearts bound ever closer to Him.

Passing on the Faith

There is another reason why prayer must remain constant in the midst of our busy lives. You will recall from chapter 2 the letter my father wrote to me during a time when I had taken on enormous occupational responsibilities and commitments. That message was to have a sweeping influence on my life.

His words, written without accusation or insult, hit me like the blow from a hammer. It is possible for mothers and fathers to love and revere God while systematically losing their children. You can go to church three times a week, serve on its governing board, attend the annual picnic, and pay your tithes. But if you do not combine fervent prayer with these activities, you may still fail to pass on your faith and beliefs to the next generation.

The urgency of this mission has taken Shirley and me to our knees since before the birth of our first child. From October 1971 until early 1978, I designated one day a week for fasting and prayer specifically devoted to the spiritual welfare of our children. Shirley then accepted the responsibility and continues it to this day. This commitment springs from an intense awareness of our need for divine assistance in the awesome task of parenthood.

I'm told that George McCluskey, my great-grandfather on the maternal side, carried a similar burden for his children through the final decades of his life. He invested the hour from eleven to twelve o'clock each morning in intercessory prayer for his children and for future generations of his family. Toward the end of his life, he announced that God had made him a promise: Every member of four generations of his family would become Christians.

That promise has been working itself out in remarkable ways. By the time I came along, every family member from my great-grandfather to me not only had accepted Christ, but also had been or were ministers. H. B. London, my cousin and a member of the fourth generation, is also a minister. I am the only one who did not feel specifically called to this service. Yet considering the hundreds of times I have talked to audiences about the gospel of Christ, I feel like an honorary member of the team!

I fully understand that when responsibilities and activities pile one on top of another, it is easy to let your commitment to daily prayer begin to slide. I suggest, however, that you reexamine your schedule in order to make prayer for your children your first priority. There is no higher calling on the face of this earth.

Peace Amidst the Turmoil

When I was two years old, my family lived in a one-bedroom apartment in Sulphur Springs, Texas. My tiny bed sat right beside that of my parents. It was common then for my father to awaken at night to an anxious little voice whispering, "Daddy? Daddy?"

My father would answer, "What, Jimmy?"

And I would say, "Hold my hand!"

Dad would reach across the darkness and grope for my small hand, finally engulfing it in his own. He said that the instant he had my hand firmly in his grip, my arm became limp, my breathing deep and regular. I'd immediately gone back to sleep. All I needed was to know that he was there.

Today, as grown-up mothers and fathers who are frantically attempting to meet the demands of jobs, school, church, *and* parenthood, we need the same thing. To call out in the darkness…to hear that voice of assurance…to plead, "Hold my hand!" And then, with a sigh of relief, to sense the firm yet loving touch of our heavenly Father and know that He is there.

Throughout this book we have discussed ways

to reduce the pressures and commitments that cause parental burnout. But you will never be able to eliminate them all. Trials and stress are realities of life. The unexpected is always just around the corner. That is why Jesus tells us, "Come to me, all you who are weary and burdened, and I will give you rest" (Matthew 11:28).

One of the ironies of the Christian life is that in the times of our greatest turmoil, we may discover the deepest sense of inner peace and rest—*if* we release our burdens to Him in prayer. Scripture also says, "Don't worry about anything; instead, pray about everything. Tell God what you need, and thank him for all he has done. If you do this, you will experience God's peace, which is far more wonderful than the human mind can understand" (Philippians 4:6–7, NLT).

Even in the midst of anxiety and stress, there *is* a quiet peace that is comforting. The "Father of compassion and the God of all comfort" (2 Corinthians 1:3) is always ready to hear our troubles and put His loving arms around us. He is waiting patiently for us to call upon Him.

Overwhelmed?
Solution #7
Find Peace Through Prayer

- When you are busy and stressed, do you find yourself praying more often or less?

- Make a list of the ways the Lord has calmed and comforted you during times of turmoil.

- If you are not already doing so, make time every day for the next week to pray specifically for each member of your family.

Epilogue

I hope that you have found inspiration and practical help within the pages of this book. The daily stresses of living are taxing enough; when the responsibilities of parenthood are added to your list, you have one of the toughest jobs in the world. I know—I've been there!

For easy reference, here is a list of the seven solutions to parental burnout that we have discussed:

1. Renew the Sabbath
2. Just Say "No" to Overcommitment
3. Let Go of the Desire to Acquire

4. Seek Balance for Your Life and Family
5. Turn Off Distractions and Tune In to Your Loved Ones
6. Lift Up One Another
7. Find Peace Through Prayer

In reality, there are many choices you can make to ease your burden. The most important choice, however, is to seek the Lord's answers for every problem or crisis you encounter. It was the prophet Jeremiah who wrote, "'For I know the plans I have for you,' declares the LORD, 'plans to prosper you and not to harm you, plans to give you a hope and a future'" (Jeremiah 29:11). The Lord's wisdom and ways are always your best answer.

I wish all of God's blessings to you and your precious family.

James Dobson

Notes

1. Wayne Muller, *Sabbath: Restoring the Sacred Rhythm of Rest* (New York, NY: Bantam, 1999).

2. C. H. Spurgeon, *Lectures to My Students* (Grand Rapids, MI: Zondervan Publishers, 1954), 160.

3. Adapted from Gary Rosberg, *Guard Your Heart* (Sisters, OR: Multnomah Publishers, Inc., 1994).

4. Dr. Joseph Procaccini and Mark W. Kiefaber, *Parent Burnout* (New York, NY: Doubleday & Company, Inc., 1987).

5. Marilyn Gardner, "Mothers who choose to stay home," *The Christian Science Monitor,* 14 November 2001. http://www.csmonitor.com/atcsmonitor/specials/women/home/home111401.html (accessed 24 November 2003).

6. Penny Edgell Becker, The Religion and Family Project, Hartford Institute for Religion Research, 2000. http://hirr.hartsem.edu/research/family_Becker-projectindex.html (accessed 1 December 2003).

7. Susan Lang, "Study: Couples scale back work to care for families, make time for themselves," *Cornell Chronicle,* 16 December 1999. http://www.news.cornell.edu/Chronicle/99/12.16.99/scaling_back.html (accessed 1 December 2003).

8. Leslie Haggin Geary, "I quit!" *CNNMoney,* 30 December 2003. http://money.cnn.com/2003/11/11/pf/q_iquit (accessed 4 February 2004).

9. "A Nation in Debt," *All Things Considered,* National Public Radio, 2003. http://www.npr.org/programs/atc/features/2003/jan/debt (accessed 8 December 2003).

10. As quoted in Randy Alcorn, *The Treasure Principle* (Sisters, OR: Multnomah Publishers, Inc., 2001), 50.

11. A. W. Tozer, "The Blessedness of Possessing Nothing," in *The Pursuit of God,* Bibleteacher.org. http://www.bibleteacher.org/tozchp2.htm (accessed 27 February 2004).

12. Peggy Patten, "Hurried Children, Busy Families," NPIN Parent News for Fall 2002. http://npin.org/pnews/2002/pnew902/feat902.html (accessed 10 December 2003).

13. University of Michigan Institute for Social Research, as reported by Cox News Service, 26 July 2000.

14. David Noonan, "Stop Stressing Me," *Newsweek,* 29 January 2001, 54.

15. Bob DeMoss, *TV: The Great Escape* (Wheaton, IL: Crossway Books, 2001), 33–4.

16. N. Gross, "The Entertainment Glut," *Business Week,* 16 February 1998, as reported in "Media Use in America," *Mediascope,* 5 November 2003. http://www.mediascope.org/pubs/ibriefs/mua.htm (accessed 15 December 2003).

17. L. Goodstein and M. Connelly, "Teenage Poll Finds Support for Tradition,"*New York Times,* 30 April 1998, as reported in "Media Use in America," *Mediascope,* 5 November 2003. http://www.mediascope.org/pubs/ibriefs/mua.htm (accessed 15 December 2003).

18. Kaiser Family Foundation and Children's Digital Media Centers study, as reported in "Too Much TV?" *KOMO television news report,* 29 October 2003. http://www.komotv.com/healthwatch/story.asp?ID=2 8013 (accessed 15 December 2003).

19. George Barna, *Generation Next* (Ventura, CA: Regal Books, 1995), 55.

20. B. S. Bowden and J. M. Zeisz, "Supper's On! Adolescent Adjustment and Frequency of Family Mealtimes," paper presented at 105th Annual Meeting of the American Psychological Association, Chicago, 1997.

21. *TV Guide,* 22–28 August 1992.

22. C. A. Anderson and K. E. Dill, "Video Games and Aggressive Thoughts, Feelings, and Behavior in the Laboratory and in Life," *Journal of Personality and Social Psychology,* 2000, 74, as reported in "Media Use in America," *Mediascope,* 5 November 2003. http://www.mediascope.org/pubs/ibriefs/mua.htm (accessed 15 December 2003).

23. Bob DeMoss, *TV: The Great Escape* (Wheaton, IL: Crossway Books, 2001).

STRAIGHT TALK TO MEN
In this classic book, Dr. James Dobson shows the difference between the world's perspective and God's perspective of manhood, giving you the information you need to build a strong home.

ISBN 1-59052-356-3

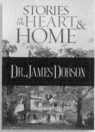

STORIES OF THE HEART AND HOME
With these collected anecdotes from Dr. Dobson's bestselling books, you'll find more than encouragement—you'll discover how to deal with real adversity, thrive in your relationships, and live with peace and purpose.

ISBN 1-59052-371-7

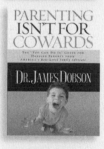

PARENTING ISN'T FOR COWARDS
Let's face it, raising children is often difficult, especially in this shock-wave world. Dr. James Dobson helps parents navigate the passage from early childhood through adolescence.

ISBN 1-59052-372-5

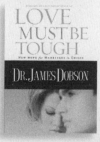

LOVE MUST BE TOUGH
In this popular classic, Dr. Dobson offers practical solutions for holding your marriage together when it appears to be falling apart. The principles of respect and "tough love" can rekindle romance at home and restore your relationship.

ISBN 1-59052-355-5

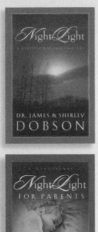

NIGHT LIGHT FOR COUPLES
This award-winning daily devotional from Dr. James and Shirley Dobson brings you personal, practical, and biblical insights that will renew your marriage—tonight and every night.

ISBN 1-57673-674-1

NIGHT LIGHT FOR PARENTS
The Dobsons follow up their original bestselling devotional with another Gold Medallion winner. Discover a daily dose of practical, personal, and spiritual insights for parenting children of all ages.

ISBN 1-57673-928-7

LOVE FOR A LIFETIME
This bestselling Gold Medallion winner has brought hope, harmony, and healing to millions of homes worldwide. With an emphasis on early marriage—especially the first ten years—this book gives men and women powerful and biblical insights for building lasting marital harmony.

ISBN 1-59052-087-4

CERTAIN PEACE IN UNCERTAIN TIMES
Fight violence, hunger, disease, and death—on your knees! National Day of Prayer Task Force chairman Shirley Dobson shows you how to nurture a true and lasting lifestyle of prayer.

ISBN 1-59052-087-4